T5-CAO-801

THE AMERICAN ALLIGATOR
Its Life in the Wild

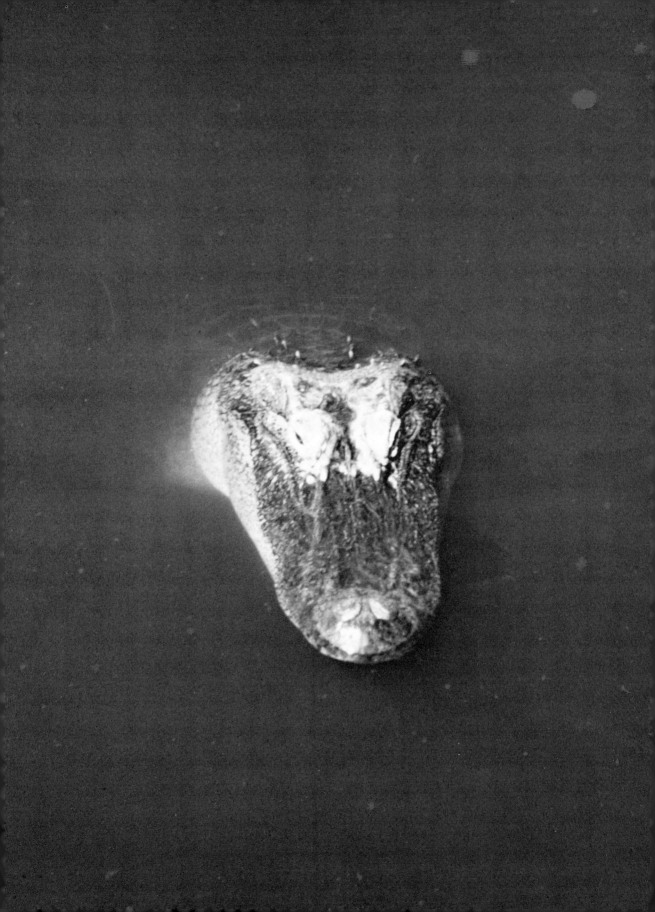

THE AMERICAN ALLIGATOR
Its Life in the Wild

by Edward R. Ricciuti

Illustrated with photographs

Harper & Row, Publishers
New York, Evanston, San Francisco, London

THE AMERICAN ALLIGATOR
Its Life in the Wild

Library of Congress Catalog Card Number: 72-76502

Trade Standard Book Number: 06-024995-1
Harpercrest Standard Book Number: 06-024996-X

FIRST EDITION

To my grandparents

Contents

Acknowledgments

*Many dedicated scientists and conservationists helped with information
in preparation of this book, and in reading parts of the manuscript.
I would like to thank especially Dr. F. Wayne King, Curator of
Herpetology and Chairman of Educational Programs of the New York
Zoological Society; John Ogden, biologist at the Everglades
National Park; and Ted Joanen, Research Leader, Refuge Division,
Louisiana Wildlife and Fisheries Commission.*

THE AMERICAN ALLIGATOR
Its Life in the Wild

Introduction

The cool dusk of a spring evening gathers over the brown swamp water. For just a moment, it seems as if the beat of life in the swamp has hushed. But as night falls, the swamp sounds start again. The "jug-o'-rum" calls of the bullfrogs boom amid the lily pads. From hidden places in clumps of grass rises the trilling call of the chorus frogs. They are tiny. Each is only about an inch long. Yet their calling fills the night air.

Mist is forming above the quiet pools of water. The mist sends out fingers that curl around the cypress trees. Overhead, the snowy egrets flap like silent ghosts through the darkening sky. They wheel toward a tall stand of cypress trees. In a flurry of white plumes, the egrets settle down. With golden feet they grasp the branches on which they will roost for the night.

Meanwhile, the black-crowned night herons are winging to their feeding grounds. Every so often a harsh croak from above tells of their passing. This is the time when the night herons stalk through the shallows. They snatch up fish and crayfish with the ends of their long bills.

On the island where the cypress trees grow, a tiny creature is moving through the low grass. It is a least shrew, a relative of the

3

moles. It weighs no more than two dimes. It is no longer than one of your fingers. But in its tiny world the shrew is a relentless hunter. Much of its life is spent scurrying about looking for something to eat. And the shrew eats almost any other animal it can kill, including insects, worms, and lizards. Although fierce, the shrew is so tiny it does not disturb the whitetail deer that stands nearby. The deer is smaller than its relatives in the north. Its head moves from side to side as its brown eyes scan the darkness. Suddenly the deer's ears twitch. It listens to a mighty sound that explodes from some hidden corner of the swamp.

It is a sound that thundered over the swamplands long before man walked the earth. Somewhere in the wilderness of water and thicket, an American alligator has begun to bellow. The roar of the alligator seems to shake the swamp. To people who know the swamp and the alligator, this sound has a special meaning. It signals that the time has come for the male and female alligators to mate. By the end of the summer young alligators, black with yellow markings, will swim in the brown swamp water. Another chapter will begin in the story of the alligator. It is a tale as old as the dinosaurs.

Lying motionless in the water, the American alligator is well camouflaged.

The History of the Alligator

The American alligator is a large animal. Male alligators some-times reach fifteen feet or more in length, although such big males are rare. Female alligators are smaller. They seldom grow beyond nine feet long. Adult alligators are black and covered with horny scales which are rectangular in shape. The scales are arranged in rows and linked by tough skin. Lying in the water, with its black, rough hide, the alligator closely resembles a floating log. The back of the alligator's head is armored with heavy plates of bone. Its belly is light in color.

Although it lives both in water and on land, the American alli-gator is particularly suited to life in the water. Its feet are webbed. Its tail is flattened on the sides. The alligator swims by sweeping its tail like an oar from side to side. While swimming, the alligator holds its feet and legs close to its body.

The eyes and nostrils of an alligator are above the plane of its head. This permits the alligator to lie with most of its body in the water and yet continue to breathe and look around. When the alligator dives, two flaps of muscle in each nostril clamp shut, so no water enters the animal's nostrils. Other flaps close over the alligator's ears. The alligator also has a third eyelid that is used underwater. The eyelid, a transparent membrane, closes over the alligator's eye. No water penetrates the membrane, but it is clear enough for the alligator to see through in the water.

The alligator is a predator. It preys on other animals for food. The alligator often seizes its prey in its mouth under the water. When this happens, of course, water enters the alligator's mouth. If the alligator swallowed a great deal of water, it could drown. But the alligator does not swallow the water. A valve in the alligator's throat closes, walling off the mouth from the windpipe. This valve also allows the alligator to hold prey in its mouth at the surface and to continue to breathe.

Alligators swim by sculling their tails to and fro in the water.

The jaws of the alligator, which end in a broad, round snout, are suited to crushing prey, such as turtles. The upper jaw extends stiffly from the alligator's skull. It is not hinged and cannot move separately from the rest of the skull. The lower jaw, however, is hinged and can move. Each jaw is armed with about forty teeth set in sockets.

Like other reptiles, the alligator is a cold-blooded creature. It does not produce its own body heat. Instead, the temperature of the alligator's body is determined by the temperature of its surroundings. If the alligator is cold, it must move into the sun. If it is warm, it must seek the shade.

When an alligator bellows, it lifts its head from the water.

The alligator belongs to a group of animals called the Crocodilians. Scientists call groups like the Crocodilians "orders." The order of Crocodilians, scientifically known as the *Crocodilia,* has the same ancestors the dinosaurs had. The Crocodilians, in fact, are the closest living relatives of the dinosaurs.

Scientists divide the Crocodilians into three smaller groups, called "families." One family is the crocodiles. There are sixteen different kinds of crocodiles living today. They live in both fresh and salt water throughout many of the warm parts of the world.

Another family of Crocodilians has only one living member. It is the Indian gharial, also known as gavial. The gharial has a long, thin snout. Its teeth are like spikes. They can hold wriggly prey. The teeth are an advantage for the gharial, which feeds largely on fish.

The alligators and caimans make up the remaining family, called *Alligatoridae,* of the Crocodilians. There are nine kinds of caimans, all living in Central and South America. Two species of true alligator exist today. The Chinese alligator, which is very rare, lives in the Yangtze Kiang River basin of China. People often ask how to tell the difference between an alligator and a crocodile. The easiest way to tell just by looking is to see whether the fourth tooth on the lower jaw is out or in when the jaws are closed. In crocodiles, the tooth can be seen. This tooth in alligators, however, lodges in a space inside the jaws and cannot be seen when they are shut. The American alligator lives only in the southeastern United States. Scientists have given it the scientific name *Alligator mississippiensis.* Since pioneer times, however, the alligator has been known in the South simply as the "gator."

The story of the American alligator and its relatives begins very long ago. It has been traced back more than 180 million years, to the dawn of the Age of Reptiles. This was the age known as the Triassic period. For millions of years beginning with the Triassic, reptiles were the most successful animals on the earth.

9 During the Triassic there lived an order of reptiles which we

Several of the alligator's teeth become quite large with age. Very old alligators, however, lose most of their teeth.

now call Thecodonts. Thecodont comes from the Greek words for "socket" and "tooth." The Thecodonts had teeth that were set in sockets of the jawbone. So have the Crocodilians and the mammals, including man. The Thecodonts were not huge animals. Probably the biggest were about fifteen or twenty feet long. They had hind legs that were stronger than their front legs. This suggests that the Thecodonts walked on their hind legs. By running in great strides, the Thecodonts must have caught the smaller reptiles on which they fed. As ages passed, the Thecodonts died out. But they left

10

descendants. Among these descendants were the dinosaurs—and the Crocodilians.

The first Crocodilians looked and behaved much like their Thecodont ancestors. Some of the earliest Crocodilians had hind legs that were much longer than their front legs. They probably ran down their prey on land. As millions of years passed, some of the Crocodilians began to change. They started to look like the Crocodilians of today. At the same time their habits also changed. Slowly the Crocodilians became suited to life in the water.

During the Age of Reptiles, some dinosaurs reached great size. So did some of the Crocodilians. One ancient crocodile was more than fifty feet long, twice the length of any kind of Crocodilian living today. This huge creature probably waited at the edges of streams and lakes to prey on small dinosaurs.

About seventy million years ago, at the end of the Cretaceous period, the Age of Reptiles ended. It did not end quickly. Changes slowly occurred which made it harder for many reptiles to live. One important change was that the climate became cooler and drier. Other changes may have happened, too—we cannot be sure. But there came a day when the earth was different from what it had been before. The last dinosaur had tumbled into the dust. Many kinds of Crocodilians, too, had disappeared.

When the Age of Reptiles ended, only three lines of Crocodilians remained. From these developed the three families of living Crocodilians. There are many reasons, some of them complex, why they survived and other Crocodilians did not. The ancestors of the modern Crocodilians were large, but not giant. They spent most of the time in the water, where they found plenty of fish and other water animals to eat. The truly giant Crocodilians, on the other hand, needed very special conditions and larger prey, such as smaller dinosaurs. When the conditions changed and the prey died out, so did the giant Crocodilians.

Meanwhile, the mammals had taken over the land. They adapted more quickly than the reptiles. Those Crocodilians of the Age of

Reptiles that still lived largely on land could not compete with the mammals for food and living space. These Crocodilians too disappeared. But only a few mammals took to the water, and these took up different niches from the Crocodilians. Therefore, they did not compete with Crocodilians that were at home in lakes, streams, and swamps. These are some of the reasons why today the crocodile, gharial, and alligator families still inhabit many of the earth's wet places.

The alligator family began in either Asia or North America. Fossils of ancient alligators have been found on both continents. Either the family spread from North America, or the other way around. At any rate, millions of years before man appeared, at least three different kinds of alligator lived in North America. Some of these ancient alligators lived in what are now the Western Plains states. This region, now dry, was warm, moist, and covered with hot, steamy swampland. At the same time, the species that probably was the ancestor of the American alligator was wallowing in the swamps of Florida and other parts of the Southeast. Conditions over a great part of North America were just right for the alligators. They thrived.

However, conditions did not remain the same, at least not in the western region. In ways big and small, the earth always is changing. This means that the environment on which a species of animal depends may change radically as time passes. If an animal cannot cope with the changes, it becomes extinct. This, of course, happened to the dinosaurs. It also happened to the alligators living in western North America. There the climate slowly became more dry. Grasslands replaced the swamps and marshes where the alligators lived. As their homes disappeared, the alligators vanished too. In southeastern North America, however, the climate remained moist. The ancestor of the American alligator did not lose its home. It survived. Its descendants became the gators of today.

Only the cold winters in the north and the dry lands to the west bounded the range of the American alligator. It spread throughout the southeastern quarter of the continent. When the mammoths

12

and mastodons hulked about the landscape, the American alligator already had been here for millions of years. The bellow of the gator was an ancient sound in the swamp by the time man arrived in North America to hunt the mammoth. For ages, the life of the American alligator remained much as it had been in the past. But very suddenly, not long ago, it changed drastically.

The American Indian had lived with the gator for uncounted thousands of years without disturbing its ancient way of life. However, the coming of European settlers to gator country meant that never again would the life of the alligator be the same. The name "alligator" comes from the Spanish words "el lagarto," for "the lizard." This was the name the early Spanish explorers of the Southeast gave the alligator.

At the time the first American settlers moved into the Southeast, the alligator lived from the Atlantic seaboard to eastern Texas and Oklahoma, and from southern Virginia to the southern tip of Florida. Gators bellowed in the Dismal Swamp on the border of Virginia and North Carolina. They followed the rivers into the flatlands of Texas. Travelers on Mississippi riverboats watched gators in the water as far north as the middle of Arkansas.

Not only did the American alligator range over a wide area, but it was the most numerous large wild animal in most of its region. The gator numbered in the millions. Hardly a marsh or swamp was without alligators. William Bartram, a colonial naturalist, observed alligators in Florida from 1774 to 1776. He wrote of the incredible numbers of alligators he found. They were so numerous in Florida's St. Johns River, Bartram said, "that it would have been easy to have walked across on their heads." The alligator would not long remain so plentiful. Even by the time Bartram visited Florida a slaughter of alligators had begun.

At first, only a few gators were killed now and then by trappers, hunters, and settlers. Some people killed alligators because they feared the big reptiles. Other gator hunters were after the tasty meat of the alligator's tail. Even so, not really large numbers of gators were killed. Before the end of the eighteenth century, how-

13

ever, there was another reason to kill the American alligator. Boots, saddlebags, and other items made of alligator hide had become fashionable. When tanned, alligator hide, particularly from the gator's belly, makes a beautiful leather. It can be fashioned into belts, shoes, suitcases, handbags, and many other products.

The demand for alligator leather products increased. Alligator hunters could make great profits by selling hides to the tanneries. The tanneries shipped the finished leather from the United States to all over the world. So gator hunters poled flatboats into the swamps where the reptiles lived. On horseback, the hunters patrolled riverbanks, alert for gators floating in the water. With rifle, pistol, club, and axe, the hunters slaughtered the alligators.

The hunters were especially successful at night. Alligators are very active after the sun goes down. Cloaked by darkness, an alligator is like a will-o'-the-wisp, very difficult to see. But if light is shone into the eyes of an alligator, they betray its hiding place. This is because the eyes of the alligator, like those of many other animals active at night, show eyeshine. When the light of a torch or lamp is beamed at the eyes of an alligator, it is reflected and the eyes stand out like red coals burning in the blackness.

Eyeshine results from the way light acts on a special layer of cells, called the tapetum, in the eye of the animal. In all animals, light entering the eye is picked up by the retina, which lies behind the eyeball. The retina in the eye acts like the film in a camera. It absorbs light. Some light, however, escapes. It passes through the retina and is lost. In animals with the tapetum, however, the retina has another chance to catch the light that has escaped. The tapetum mirrors the light that passes through the retina. The light is bounced back through the retina, where it can be absorbed. In this way the eye picks up extra light that normally would not register on the retina. This is a great advantage for an animal that goes about its business at night, when light is scarce. But it is a disadvantage to animals that are the targets of hunters, for it causes eyeshine.

Once an alligator is sighted by a hunter it can be killed easily.　14

Although the alligator is powerful and agile in the water, it is no match for a man with a gun or a hatchet, on land or in a boat.

At first there were so many alligators that hunting them was a quick way to earn money. Moreover, alligator leather was not a passing fad of fashion. Year after year, its popularity continued. So, therefore, did the killing of alligators. By the year 1900 more than two and a half million alligators had been killed in Florida. As many had been destroyed by hunters in Louisiana. Throughout the rest of the Southeast the story was the same. Gator hide meant easy money. Almost nowhere was the alligator safe from the bullets, clubs and axes of the gator hunters.

As the twentieth century progressed, the slaughter increased. The alligator appeared doomed. During the ten years between 1930 and 1940 between one and two million alligators were killed in Florida; elsewhere the situation was just as bad. However, the hunters began to have problems. They had killed so many alligators that the reptiles had become very scarce. They had vanished from regions that had been their homes for millions of years. In many places where alligators once were numerous, they could be seen only in protected parks and refuges, so even where alligators remained, their numbers were just a fraction of what they had been. Big alligators rarely were seen—the hunters had killed almost all of them. With the larger alligators difficult to find, the hunters began killing the smaller ones.

Meanwhile, other forces were at work against the alligator. Men drained and filled the swamps and marshes to make farmlands and housing sites. The waste of homes and industries polluted the waters. Destruction of the place where a wild animal lives kills it as surely as a bullet. For that matter, a few members of a species may escape the hunters. But when a wild creature's home is destroyed, there is no escape.

As the alligator became more and more scarce, the value of its hide increased. A foot of alligator hide was worth less than a dollar at the beginning of this century. By 1969, it was valued at more

15

than $8.00 a foot. This made gator hunting even more profitable, although there were fewer alligators. Meanwhile, however, conservationists had begun to call attention to the danger that alligators would soon be extinct. Midway through the 1960's, the number of alligators had reached a dangerous low point. In all of Louisiana there were less than 40,000 gators. Mississippi had only 3,000 of them. Alabama was the home of only about 6,000 of the big reptiles. And in these states and elsewhere the numbers were dropping quickly. One at a time, the states where the alligator lived passed laws against hunting it. They also began to arrest people who broke these laws.

Unfortunately, these laws did not stop all of the gator hunters. Instead, they began to operate secretly. When hunting was legal, at least it was controlled by law, but poachers operated entirely outside the law. Not even the alligators in protected places such as the Everglades National Park were safe. Rangers there had to keep a constant watch over the park's alligators. Despite the laws passed in the southern states, alligator hunting continued. The hides

The hide of the alligator can be made into one of the finest leathers. Poachers become rich selling alligator hides.

stripped from dead alligators by hunters continued to arrive at leather tanneries. Most of the tanneries were located in New York City and other parts of the Northeast. Here, too, were the centers of fashion that promoted the use of alligator leather.

Alarmed conservationists and groups of citizens asked for stronger laws against illegal gator hunting. The United States government began to watch for shipments of illegal alligator hides. The government also, in 1969, placed the alligator on its official list of endangered wildlife in the United States. Near the end of 1969 New York City passed a law that helped slow the alligator's slide to extinction. It forbade trade in alligator products. This meant that hunters in the South could not sell as many hides to northern buyers. If the hides could not be used in the fashion industry, the hunters would have almost no one to whom they could sell hides, and therefore would stop hunting the gator. Within a few months, New York State also forbade the alligator-products trade, and other states followed. Meanwhile, the southeastern states toughened laws against alligator hunting, so at the same time, it had become more risky to break the laws against hunting. For the first time in more than a century, some of the hunting stopped.

The alligator came back in surprisingly short time. Alligators began to turn up in ponds, canals, and marshes, where they had not been seen for years. Left alone, the older alligators could breed. Young alligators were seen more often. By 1971, more than one million alligators were alive in the wild. Several hundred thousand were in Louisiana; and a similar number lived in Florida. Alligators remained in Georgia, Texas and other parts of gator country. Many people had feared that the alligator had been close to extinction. But the gator began to make the slow climb back.

Gator Country

American alligators are still missing from much of the region they once inhabited. In many other parts of gator country only pockets of alligators remain, instead of the millions that once lived there. While alligators are found over a vast region, they are missing from many areas within that region. The boundaries of the gator's range have also shrunk. Alligators no longer live as far north as the Dismal Swamp. Nor are they found as far up the Mississippi River or as far west as in the past.

Even so, alligators still inhabit a vast part of the southeastern United States. Gator country stretches from North Carolina south through Florida. It extends from the Atlantic coast to eastern Texas and possibly into a speck of southeastern Oklahoma. This does not mean that alligators are found everywhere throughout this region. In Alabama and Georgia, alligators inhabit the southern half of the state. A small part of southern Arkansas holds all that is left of that state's gators. Almost all of the alligators in South Carolina inhabit the coastal plain region. In North Carolina, the few alligators that remain are mostly in the South. The alligators of Mississippi live largely in the southern part of the state and north along the Mississippi River. The alligators of Texas live in a strip of country that

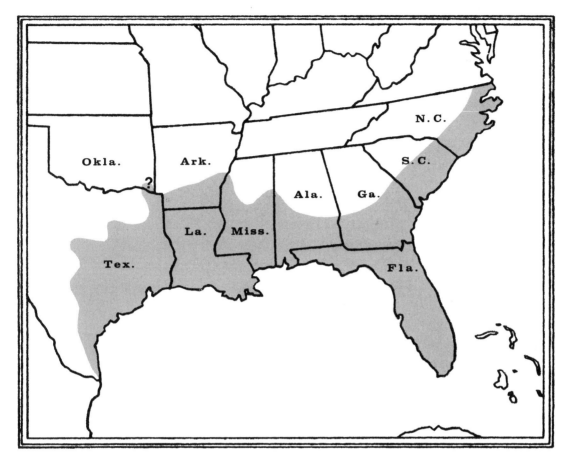

The shaded area shows the present-day range of the American alligator.

runs west of Louisiana through central Texas. Large numbers of alligators do live in Florida and Louisiana. They can be seen throughout most of these states.

Because the land of the alligator covers so much territory, however, alligators live under many different conditions. In the more northern parts of gator country, winters are chilly. In the southern parts, they are not. Some parts of the alligator's range have yearly droughts, while others rarely do. Moreover, alligators make their homes in many kinds of places: rivers, creeks, sloughs, ponds,

19

lakes, canals, and marshes, both fresh and salt. Some live far inland, miles from the sea. Others live on islands off the Gulf Coast. Some live in wildernesses. Others live in ponds in towns and cities.

These differences mean that alligators do not have all of the same habits everywhere. It is true that all American alligators share a way of life that belongs to the gator alone. Every species of animal in nature has its own special pattern of living. But this overall pattern is shaped by the conditions under which an animal lives. These may cause some changes in the pattern. An alligator of the Everglades, which dry up yearly, has some habits unlike those of a gator living in a Georgia river where water runs all year. Even so, there are many things that can be said about all alligators—and about all of the places where alligators make their homes.

The home of the American alligator is the wetlands of the Southeast. The alligator shares the wetlands with a vast number of animals and plants, large and small. All depend on the wetlands. Together, all form the web of life in the wetlands. And every plant and animal of the web has an important part in it.

THE EVERGLADES

Some of the wetlands of the Southeast are very well known. The most well-known of these are the Everglades. The words Everglades and alligator seem to go together. Probably more people think of the Everglades than any other place when they hear the word alligator. No one is certain how many alligators live in the Everglades; it is likely that most of Florida's gators are found there.

The Everglades are one of the world's largest freshwater marshes. Two thousand square miles of the marsh are in Everglades National Park. Yet this is only one sixth of the original Everglades: Outside the park three thousand square miles remain. Many more thousands of square miles have been drained for farm- 20 land. The Everglades cover much of south Florida. They begin at Lake Okeechobee in the middle of the southern part of the state. From the lake, the Everglades extend one hundred miles to the south and southwest. In places, they stretch from the Gulf of Mexico almost to Florida's east coast, and are up to sixty miles wide.

The landscape of the Everglades is as flat as a dinner plate. Its highest point is only twenty-five feet above sea level. From Lake Okeechobee it tilts very slightly to the southwest, toward the Gulf. The Everglades are based on lime rock which was once under the sea. The rock is filled with fossils of ancient sea creatures. In many parts of the Everglades, the rock is covered by peat, the remains of plants that partially decayed ages ago. In other places, however, the bare rock, beige-white in color, gleams in the sunlight.

The Everglades are often pictured as a dark, dank swamp. True, there are patches of swamp within the Everglades. Mostly, however, the Everglades are a land of great spaces, light, and wide horizons. The heart of the Everglades is a region of vast, flooded prairies. These the Indians long ago named the "grassy water." The

The Everglades are not a dark swampland, but rather a vast, open freshwater marsh.

Hammocks of high ground form islands in the midst of the sea of saw grass.

prairies are covered with a tall sedge called saw grass. Its blades are edged with tiny spines so sharp that if rubbed the wrong way they cause deep cuts.

The saw grass in the Everglades grows tall, often twice as high as a man. It bends in the wind that seems always to sweep across the glades. In some places the saw grass stretches as far as the eye can see. On clear days, the saw-grass prairie meets a deep blue sky on the horizon. Overhead, puffy white clouds sail by. Their shadows pass over the waving grass below. Here and there amid the saw grass rise tree islands called hammocks. Some of the hammocks are small, just dots of dark green in the sea of grass. Others are as big as, or bigger than, a football field. On the hammocks, trees and bushes grow green and thick. Live oak, mahogany, and

22

gumbo-limbo grow on the higher hammocks. On hammocks that are flooded part of the year, red bay, willow, and buttonbush grow in a tangle laced by the thick roots of the strangler fig. Air plants—plants which do not root in the ground—perch on the branches of the trees. The ground is carpeted with ferns.

Between some of the islands are channels called sloughs. Here the water runs deep. White water lilies dot the surface of the water. In some places tall cypress trees, bearded with Spanish moss, grow along the sloughs.

In much of the Everglades, the saw grass is mixed with other marsh plants. Here and there are patches of pickerelweed, with violet-blue flowers and heart-shaped leaves. Maiden cane and cattails rustle with the saw grass in the breeze.

The saw grass is a freshwater plant. To the south and west, where the Everglades meet the sea, it disappears. Here the Everglades are fringed with an unusual ribbon of swamp called the mangrove wilderness.

Mangroves are evergreen trees that grow in the warm regions of the world. They live where fresh and salt water mix. This occurs near the seashore, so mangroves hug the coast. They have the coastal swamps largely to themselves—most other trees cannot survive a steady bath of salt water. Growing in shallow water, mangroves collect soil, shells and other debris in their spidery roots. In this way, islands and mud flats form around clumps of mangroves. Florida's mangrove wilderness is a maze of such islands, more than ten thousand of them. Countless channels, where water is pushed back and forth by the tides, interlace the islands. In the southern Everglades, the mangroves form a belt up to fifteen miles wide. Many boatmen have been lost there for days.

Once in the mangrove wilderness, it is easy to forget where you are. It always has seemed to me that a trip into the mangrove wilderness almost takes you back in time. The mud flats around the mangroves are black and slick. Trails across the mud tell of creatures that have scuttled out of the sea into the mangrove tangle.

23

Deep among the trees, branches rustle. Possibly the sea breeze moves them. Or possibly an animal is passing by. The Everglades have been called a place of mystery. No part of them is more mysterious than where the Everglades end and the sea begins.

Animal life in the Everglades is a mixture. Here mingle animals of the sea, fresh water, and land. The Everglades are also a meeting ground for animals from north and south. It is the home of creatures big and small. In the waters of the mangrove fringes, swarms of pink shrimp grow to adulthood. Giant tarpon, mullet, snook, 24

Wood ibises, which actually are storks, nest in the mangroves at the edge of the Everglades.

and other marine fish cruise up the creeks that wind through the mangroves. More than two hundred species of fish have been found in Everglades waters. These range from the huge and fearsome great white shark to the tiny least killifish and mosquito fish.

The mosquito fish, though guppy-size, is fierce enough in its own small world. Great numbers of mosquito fish live in the fresh waters of the Everglades. They snap at other small fish and gobble up mosquito wrigglers on the surface of the water. There are plenty of mosquitoes to go around: Fifty different kinds live in the Everglades. Catfish, bream, bass, and sunfish thrive in the sloughs and ponds. So do gars, which lie in the water in rows.

Crayfish—which are really crustaceans and not fish at all—burrow in the mud that covers the limestone. Apple snails creep up the stalks of pickerelweed to leave their eggs there.

More than three hundred species of birds rest on tree limbs, wade and paddle in the water, and fly overhead. Great blue herons and snowy egrets search for fish and other prey at the sides of sloughs and in the shallow waters. Swallow-tailed kites, black-and-white birds of prey, wheel overhead. They capture flying insects and search for frogs and snakes in the trees. The great nests of bald eagles and ospreys, built of sticks, are perched in the mangrove trees. Along the coast, skimmers dart over the water, their big bills cutting through the waves. Coots and gallinules bob in the water.

Unlike the birds, most of the mammals of the Everglades are seldom seen. Many prowl at night. Others are small or keep well hidden. But mammals are an important part of Everglades life. More than forty species inhabit the great marsh. Among the rarest is the Florida panther, called the puma in other parts of the country. This great tawny cat can weigh more than two hundred pounds. Bigger than the panther is the black bear. It is not common in the Everglades, but on rare occasions it can be seen shuffling through the brush or hammocks and pushing through the saw grass. Deer and raccoon are common throughout the area.

Florida water rats, round tails dragging behind them, build their small nests on mats of floating plants and in shallow water. River otters play in the deeper water. They and their relatives the minks hunt fish, frogs, and other small animals.

Turtles are almost everywhere. They bask on the banks of sloughs and on logs. They seem sleepy. But when an enemy nears, they disappear into the water in a twinkling. The Everglades are the home of more than sixty species of reptiles and amphibians. These include the cottonmouth and eastern diamondback rattlesnake, two of the largest venomous snakes in North America.

Two large alligators bask on the bank of a slough in the Everglades National Park.

In the Everglades, however, the alligator is king. Many alligators live in the saw-grass prairies. Others spend most of their time in and around the sloughs. And in the winter and early spring, middle-sized alligators lie in culverts that pass under dirt roads in parts of the national park. I have driven with park rangers along roads where every culvert had its alligator at home.

Although most of the big alligators in the Everglades have been killed, some very large bulls remain. I will remember always the sight of a twelve-foot bull gator floating in a small pond. The top of his back, his eyes, and part of his snout were just above the surface. Every so often, a lazy movement of his tail pushed him a few feet through the water. As I watched him with field glasses, a movement in the sky caught my eye. A bald eagle, which nested in a far-off cypress tree, swooped low over the pond. Its wing tips swept less than ten feet above the floating alligator, and I could see both

27

animals at once through my glasses. Here, in one glance, were two of our most spectacular American animals.

In years past, this sight would not have been unusual. But today it is. Both the bald eagle and the American alligator, once common, now are considered unusual sights.

Like its animals, the Everglades themselves are threatened. Much of the Everglades north of the national park have been drained for farmland. Even the marshland in the park is in danger. It no longer receives the flow of water it did in the past.

The life of the Everglades is tied forever to the coming and going of water. Lake Okeechobee, seven hundred square miles in size, is the source of the Everglades' water. For thousands and thousands of years, the Everglades have depended on water from the lake. The water has come and gone in a yearly cycle.

The weather of south Florida is subtropical. That means it has a wet-dry yearly cycle instead of a warm-cold pattern as in the north. June in south Florida is the time when the rains begin. They come with tropical fury. Gray clouds scud across the sky. Raindrops spatter on the tossing saw grass and weaving cypress branches. All summer, and into autumn, heavy rains fall frequently. And each year, as the rains have fallen, the lake has overflowed. Water from Lake Okeechobee has flowed southward over the flat prairies of the Everglades. The water forms a vast sheet over the saw-grass prairies. In some places it is only a few inches deep. Because the land slopes only slightly to the southwest, the movement of the water is hardly visible. But at this time the Everglades can be said to be covered by a great river flowing toward the gulf.

This is the way it was. The water meant life for the snails, frogs, fish, turtles, and all the other creatures of the Everglades. Hardly any rain fell in the winter. But until the spring, the water continued to spill over from the lake. This meant that for ten months a year, the Everglades gleamed under a film of life-giving water. True, in some years less rain fell than usual. Droughts did occur, parching the marshes. But eventually the rain clouds would darken the sky over the Everglades and the lake, and the drought would end. Once more water would well over from the lake into the marshes.

Then, about fifty years ago, man began to make changes in this natural cycle. The rains have continued to fall on schedule. But no longer does the water flow freely from Lake Okeechobee. In 1926 and 1928, floods caused by hurricanes swept from Lake Okeechobee and killed thousands of people. The United States Army Corps of Engineers began to dike the lake. Levees have been built. Canals have been dug. Marshes have been drained and filled. Farms and homes have replaced the saw grass. Today engineers, not nature, control the flow of water from Lake Okeechobee and in the Everglades. When droughts occur, water is diverted from the Everglades to the farmlands and cities. This makes the drought in the marshes even worse. In time of flooding, unwanted water is flushed over the Everglades. This often means that the Everglades receive too much water at one time. The balance of the yearly water cycle has been destroyed. Now conservationists, the government, and public agencies must cooperate to keep the Everglades alive.

MERRITT ISLAND

North of the Everglades, on the east coast of central Florida, huge structures rise near the sea. These are the buildings and missile sites of the John F. Kennedy Space Center. Towering rockets point toward space. Mighty machines clank across the landscape. There is a feeling of excitement here. Men already have left this place for the moon. For what far worlds will they leave it in the future? Yet almost in the shadow of the launching sites one can believe for a moment he has stepped into the past, for the quiet pools, marshes, and creeks near the space center are the home of many alligators.

Part of the grounds of the space center were set aside in 1963 as a national wildlife refuge—Merritt Island. On its west side flows

29

the wide and beautiful Indian River. To the east crash the breakers of the Atlantic Ocean. The Merritt Island refuge was set aside as a sanctuary for waterfowl that migrate from the north and winter here.

Each winter 40,000 ducks of more than twenty species settle down at Merritt Island. The ducks are joined by 100,000 coots, whose black forms seem everywhere on the water. Bald eagles soar overhead. Some bald eagles nest in the refuge during the winter. Herons and white ibis live here year-round. In all, more than 250 species of birds visit the refuge at one time or another.

The refuge consists largely of freshwater marshes, with salt creeks and lagoons. Slash pine, live oak and cabbage palm grow on higher ground. Near the salt creeks, mangrove thickets edge the water. There are many whitetail deer here, and bobcats, raccoons, opossums, and armadillos, too. The eastern diamondback rattle-snake prowls at night, and one must watch out for cottonmouths and coral snakes.

Alligators can be found throughout the refuge. No one has counted exactly how many live there, but the number is large. The alligators of Merritt Island seem to be thriving amid the bustle of the space center. They live in the marshes, creeks, and even the irrigation canals that water the orange groves on the grounds of the refuge. Their kind is ancient, although the gators have no way of knowing it. When their ancestors first saw man, he used stone tools and wore animal skins. Now man builds space centers and soars to the moon, but alligators still live much as their ancestors did. Seeing the space center and then watching alligators floating in the quiet waters of Merritt Island makes one wonder. Will the alligator outlast man? Will man leave no place on this planet for the alliga-tor? Or is there really a place in nature for man and the gator?

OKEFENOKEE

A space center seems an unlikely place to see alligators. A few hours drive north of Merritt Island is a great swamp that looks just the opposite—exactly the spot where one should see them. It is the Okefenokee, the "land of the trembling earth." The name is an Indian one, and it fits. For in the Okefenokee Swamp, the soft, peaty earth really does tremble under your feet. A look at the history of this swamp on the Georgia-Florida border will tell you why.

More than a million years ago the waves of the Atlantic Ocean rolled over much of what is now Georgia. The Atlantic in that ancient time was 150 feet above today's sea level. Surf boomed on beaches 75 miles inland from the present Georgia coastline. To the south, the Everglades had not yet appeared. A group of four small islands marked the site of what became northern Florida. Ocean currents swept past these islands. The currents, and the action of waves, slowly piled up a great sandbar. The bar was not merely a little patch of sand. It stretched for a hundred miles from north to south.

Eventually the level of the sea sank. The ocean retreated from the sandbar. The bar was left high and dry. Gradually plants took root on the bar. It became a ridge of dry land. Behind the ridge was a large but shallow bowl in the earth. A bit of the ancient sea had been trapped there as the ocean had retreated. A salt lake had formed. But the water did not stay salty: The rain made it fresh. Freshwater plants moved into the lake. When the plants died, their remains sank to the bottom. After a long time they formed peat, which filled parts of the lake. Sedges, shrubs, trees and a variety of marsh plants took root in the peat. They grew and spread. When they died and decayed they added to the peat. The lake disappeared. It had become a swamp. The Okefenokee had been born.

The Okefenokee is one of the wildest swamps in the United States. It is 38 miles long, 25 miles wide and covers 412,000 acres. Four fifths of this area are within the Okefenokee National Wildlife Refuge. The swamp itself is surrounded by sandy forests of slash pine and longleaf pine. Once you enter the swamp, however, the countryside changes. Here are deep forests of cypress trees, their branches draped with Spanish moss. The trees are rooted in peat that in some places is twenty feet thick. Because the peat is so deep, the roots of the trees never reach the solid ground far below the crust of the peat. On other pieces of ground grow maples, sweet spire, black gum, and many small shrubs. The images of the cypresses and other trees are mirrored in the water that moves slowly through the swamp. The water is stained brown by the peat.

In many parts of the swamp the water flows over prairies, forming open marsh. Here the tips of broom sedges and grasses rise above the water. They wave in the breezes that ripple the water's surface. Neverwet plants, whose leaves shed water, carpet patches of the water's surface. In the spring, water lilies bloom white and yellow. Pickerelweed flowers, purple as the far hills, mix with swamp marigolds and floating heart plants.

Here and there, great fires have burned deep holes in the peat of the prairies. Water has filled these holes. Lakes have formed. There are more than sixty lakes and many smaller ponds in the Okefenokee. Islands dot some of the lakes and the deeper waters of the prairies. Some of the islands are sandbars; others are floating chunks of peat. They move slowly with the current.

Even on what looks like solid ground, the soil squishes underfoot. Often the earth really does quiver. I have stamped on the ground in the Okefenokee and watched trees ten feet away shake. They looked as if they were rooted in gelatin.

There are parts of the Okefenokee that look like a fairyland. I found one on a morning while walking near the edge of the swamp. A quiet little pathway wound through the green leaves over a bit of solid ground. The path itself was covered with a lacy carpet of sphagnum moss. Nearby a cardinal called. Its song was liquid and seemed to ripple through the air.

In a patch of brown mud I spied some tracks. They looked like tiny elfin handprints: A raccoon had been by that way not long before. Water was still seeping into the prints. Then, from a watery prairie in the distance, a sound was carried on the wind. It was a rolling sound, low but strong. Somewhere a sandhill crane was calling.

The sandhill crane, long-legged and almost as tall as a man, is one of the many fascinating creatures of the Okefenokee. Including the crane, more than 225 species of birds can be seen in the swamp at one time or another. Ospreys nest high in the cypress trees. The dark shapes of turkey vultures and black vultures sail overhead. Red-shouldered hawks perch in low trees along the waterways. Bobwhites scurry through the brush on dry ground. Wood ducks nest in the hollow trees. Ring-necked ducks, mallards, and black ducks dabble in the water. Herons of many kinds stalk their prey as they do in other wetlands. And sometimes herring gulls soar overhead, reminding one of the ancient time when the sea covered the swamp.

The dark waters of the swamp are the home of more than three dozen species of fish. There are mosquito fish, sunfish, and some of

An alligator rests near a waterhole in the Okefenokee Swamp. The thick growth in the background is typical of some parts of the swamp.

the biggest black bass found anywhere. More than thirty-six species of mammals make their home in the Okefenokee. Round-tailed muskrats swim in the flooded prairies. The black bear, gray fox, whitetail deer and bobcat are some of the largest mammals. The least shrew, cotton mouse, and golden mouse are some of the smallest. The golden mouse shares the swamp's islands with the Florida mole, opossum and striped skunk. Now and then, the Okefenokee may have a tawny visitor from the south: Once in a great while the Florida panther may pass, like mist in the night, through the wilderness of the Okefenokee.

The Okefenokee has many of the same reptiles and amphibians as the other wetlands of the Southeast. Large eel-like salamanders called sirens swim in the peat-stained waters. Bullfrogs and pig frogs call deeply in the night. Carpenter frogs make calls that sound like the tap of workmen's hammers. Toads hop about in search of prey. In the darkness of the swamp night, the eastern diamondback rattlesnake hunts. It uses special organs in its head to help find its prey; these organs sense the heat given off by the body of the animal that the snake is after. Huge snapping turtles lurk in the swamp waters. They snatch at fish and other small water creatures within their reach. Other turtles abound. In drier parts of the swamp, the Carolina anole—the so-called "American chameleon"—scampers across tree branches. Other lizards called skinks run over the ground.

Many of these animals provide food for the alligators of the Okefenokee. The alligator is increasing in number in the swamp. More than 6,000 gators live there now. They float almost unseen in the dark waters. They bask on the banks of waterways and lie in the water under overhanging tree limbs. Away from flowing water, the alligators dig large wallows in the mud. The female gators often nest near such holes in the spring.

It is said that in ancient times the Okefenokee was the home of a fierce tribe of people. The men of the tribe were very cruel. The women were very beautiful. The Okefenokee is like that tribe— 34

This female alligator is clearing away brush in preparation for nesting in the Okefenokee.

cruel and beautiful. The tribe, if it ever lived, is gone. But the alligators, other ancient dwellers of the Okefenokee, remain in the land of the trembling earth.

ROCKEFELLER REFUGE

Louisiana rivals Florida as the state with the most alligators. Some of the alligators in Louisiana live in inland swamps, lakes, streams, and bayous, but most Louisiana gators spend their lives in coastal marshes. Scientists believe more than 170,000 gators live there. From the Texas border to the mouth of the Mississippi River, the coast of Louisiana is fringed with a vast marshland. Mile after mile of marsh stretches to the horizon. The marshes surround the many bays, lakes and channels. All in all, the marshes cover four million acres. Here the land and sea fade into one another. It is difficult to tell where the land ends and the Gulf of Mexico begins.

Some parts of the marsh are tidal. For a portion of each day as the tide rises they are claimed by the sea. When the tide retreats, the marshes become land once more. Heading in from the gulf, in most places one first comes upon salt marsh. Along most of the coast except in the west, a ribbon of salt marsh edges the seaward side of the entire marshland. Here oyster grass and salt grass wave in the sea wind. The tubelike stems of black rush bend before the breeze that carries in the salt spray.

Behind the salt marsh are wetlands where the water is brackish, not as salty as sea water, but not fresh either. Wire grass and other marsh grasses grow here. Where the water is practically fresh, there are a few patches of saw grass. Farthest inland are the freshwater marshes. Some have been made by man to provide resting places for waterfowl. A thick green mat of water hyacinth covers

Waterfowl by the hundreds of thousands winter in the vast coastal marshes of Louisiana.

The coastal marshes of Louisiana are fifty miles wide in some places. The tracks across the marsh are made by tractorlike vehicles called "marsh buggies."

much of the open water. The spade-shaped leaves of pickerelweed form miniature jungles in the shallows.

Here and there in the western portion of the marshland, low sandy ridges rise above the marsh. Most of these ridges are only a few feet above the level of the marsh. But they provide enough dry land for roads, and for people to build homes and farms. Groves of oaks, their branches draped with Spanish moss, grow on some of the ridges. The oak groves form windbreaks. People who live on the ridges often build their homes on the sides of the groves away from the sea wind.

37   Much of the marshland is owned by big landholders. They lease

portions of the marshes to trappers. The trappers of Louisiana make their living selling the furs of muskrats and nutria, a large rodent of up to twenty pounds. The nutria is a native of South America, which has been introduced in Louisiana. Trapping is controlled very closely by the state. It is a big business for the local people, so both the state and the trappers take care to see that enough animals survive to keep up a good supply of furs.

Muskrats and nutria thrive in the coastal marshes. Otters play and hunt fish, frogs, shellfish, and the muskrats. Raccoons and skunks prowl the marshes at night. And people who live in the marshes say sometimes the red wolf, now almost extinct, and the puma prowl the coastal wetlands. But perhaps it is for birds that the coastal marshes of Louisiana are most famous. These marshes lie at the southernmost end of the Mississippi Flyway. This is the route over which funnel the vast numbers of birds that nest in the north central United States and central Canada. Each autumn as the trees and grasses to the north turn brown, millions of birds wing south over the Flyway. Many of these birds are waterfowl.

Flock after flock of ducks and geese settle down on the waters of the Louisiana marshes. By the time the snow is flying in the North, more than five million ducks are swimming and dabbling in the marshlands.

Amid the rich coastal marshes is the Rockefeller Refuge, which provides a winter home for more than a half million waterfowl. The refuge is operated by the state. It stretches along the seacoast for 26.5 miles. The Rockefeller Refuge reaches six miles inland, where it ends at a large sandy ridge. Most of the vegetation in the refuge is wire grass, which grows in the brackish marsh. Including the ducks and geese that winter at the refuge, more than 269 species of birds are found there at one time or another. Blue geese and snow geese, which have their young on Arctic shores, winter at the refuge. Mallards, blue-winged teal, shovelers, and many other ducks do, too. The mottled duck, a close relative of the mallard, nests there. So do black-necked stilts, black-crowned and yellow-

The brown pelican, which nests on the Louisiana coast, is endangered by pesticides in the food chain.

crowned night herons, green herons, and killdeers. Great blue herons, snowy egrets, and common egrets live throughout the marshes of the refuge. Seabirds such as laughing gulls and black skimmers wheel and dart over the waves beyond the marshes. During migrations, shorebirds skitter across the mud flats. With their long bills, they probe in the mud for food. The great horned owl and sparrow hawk wing over the windswept wire grass in search of prey.

Alligators roam throughout the refuge, even to the seaside. There they hunt crabs and other small prey in the salt marshes. However, most of the time they live a little farther inland, in the brackish marshes, waterways, and the open lakes of the freshwater marshes.

There are few places where the alligator has been studied more carefully than Rockefeller Refuge. Most of the studies have been

Scientists have found that most of the alligators at the Rockefeller Wildlife Refuge prefer to stay in the freshwater marshes.

carried out by scientists of the Louisiana Wildlife and Fisheries Commission and the Federal Bureau of Sports Fisheries and Wildlife. These studies have told us much we did not know about the life of the American alligator. But there is even more that must be learned before man can really understand the way of the gator.

The Way of the Gator

Man and gator have watched each other for thousands of years. Yet to this day, much about how the gator lives is unclear. The American alligator is in many ways a creature of mystery. Even scientists who study the alligator have questions about its way of life. One reason for this is that someone who watches alligators in southern Florida may see them splashing in a gator hole during January. Because of what he sees, he may think that all alligators are up and about in winter. But someone searching for alligators in Louisiana at the same time of year may not find any alligators at all. Instead, the reptiles may be hidden in burrows. Moreover, not even all alligators living in the same place behave in the same ways at all times. One mother alligator may guard her young from danger. A neighboring mother may leave her young without any protection.

All these differences have caused disagreement among people who study the alligator. Most of them agree, however, that it will take many years and much more study to piece together the full story of how the alligator lives. Many of the pieces will be found by those who today are young people. They may not even suspect that someday they will help us understand the life of the gator.   42

The life of any wild animal changes according to the season. The way it lives in the summer may be completely different from the way it lives in winter. Perhaps, though, the best time of year to begin the story of an animal's life is in the spring. Indeed, the spring is a time when life appears to be bursting at the seams. It is a time when new life is being created. In the north, green buds pop out from tree branches that have rattled coldly in the wind all winter long, and the caps of the skunk cabbage push up from the brown muck, wet from the spring rain. In the South, the drabness of winter has given way to greenery. Salamanders gather in quiet ponds to lay their eggs. And young raccoons and bears tumble from the dens in which they have been born. Spring in the land of the gator is a time when the swamps and marshlands echo to a special kind of thunder. It is the sound of alligators calling.

In a quiet pool, where the reflection of a buttonbush darkens the water, rests a large bull alligator. The big gator fills his lungs with air. The alligator's sides puff out slightly. Ripples fan out across the water on either side of the bull's blue-black body. Suddenly the

Alligators rise and sink in the water without apparent effort.

alligator expels the air from his lungs, and a mighty sound booms forth. We are not certain just how the sound is made. It may arise as the air from the alligator's lungs passes over folds in the animal's throat. The folds may vibrate and produce a sound. The sound builds and a deep roar explodes over the water. Almost immediately, another roar follows, then another, and another, seconds apart. The roars continue, faster and faster. Each seems louder than the one before. Soon the call of the alligator swells and echoes over the marshland. Drops of water dance on the scaly back of the big bull. All around him the surface of the pool shimmers and shakes.

The call of the gator can make your skin prickle. Sometimes a single animal bellows on and off for a half hour or more. When I have listened to it, I have thought about the time when dinosaurs stirred the swamp water. And I have wondered why the gator sends its thunder over the wet places. For a long time scientists believed that only male alligators bellow. It was thought that by bellowing, the males call their mates in the spring. Now some scientists question this idea. People have observed that female alligators also bellow. Does the female answer the male? Or is the bellow not a mating call at all? Certainly, alligators sometimes bellow at other times of year. The answers to these questions are some of the parts missing from the gator's story.

Possibly sound does help the male and female alligator find one another when it is time to mate. Maybe scent plays a part. Whatever it is that draws them together, they meet each spring, usually not before April has begun. Often they join each other in the open waters of lakes, ponds and streams. Here the male and female gator mate, as alligators have done for longer than man can remember.

Scientists at the Rockefeller Refuge have studied the breeding habits of gators for many years. They have found that male gators are not ready to breed until they are at least six feet long. The scientists at Rockefeller also observed that most, but not all, alligators there mate during late May and early June.

Shortly after the mating, they part. The male goes off to live   44 much as he did before the mating season. But the life of the female changes. She has within her the fertilized eggs that will develop into young alligators. Now she alone is responsible for carrying on her kind. To produce young she must survive to build a nest and lay her eggs. The male may die, but now that makes no difference to the young alligators. As long as the female lays eggs, and some eggs hatch, there will be more alligators in the world. And with each new alligator the chances increase that the species will continue.

It is important, therefore, that nothing disturb the female's way of life after mating. Only recently, however, have we been learning what happens to the female after she and the male part. One reason this has been possible is that scientists now have the use of very small radio transmitters. The transmitters are sturdy, and strong enough to make a signal that can be received over a long distance. Yet they are very small. One can be fastened to an animal without interfering with the animal's normal living habits. The animal can be traced by tracking the signal from the radio it carries. In this way, scientists can tell where the animal goes without having to keep it in sight. They can learn how far and how fast the animal travels. They can find out where it goes at different times of day or year. They can discover in which kinds of habitats it spends most of its time.

For a number of years scientists have attached radios to female alligators in the Rockefeller Refuge. They have used a radio transmitter small enough to be mounted on a waterproof rubberized collar. The collar goes around the alligator's neck. To hold it in place, holes are drilled in the hard, bony plates behind the neck. The collar is wired to the alligator through the holes. This does not harm the alligator. The transmitter in the collar is powered by batteries and sends out a beeping signal. It can be picked up over a range of one and a half miles. Once the transmitter is operating, the alligator is released so scientists can track it.

Of course, before a radio is placed on an alligator, the animal must be found and caught. With a creature as big and strong as the alligator, this is a rugged job. It takes patience and strength. And it takes enough courage to brave the threat of snapping jaws and hammer blows of a powerful tail.

It is not too difficult, however, to creep up behind a sleeping or resting alligator. If the gator is not startled, a noose at the end of a long pole can be slipped over its snout and back to the neck. Once the noose is around the gator's neck it is tightened. Then the battle is on. The alligator lunges and thrashes about. Men and alligator slip and splash in the water. More nooses and ropes are tossed over the alligator. In the end, the alligator is bound fast, its feet firmly lashed, and its jaws tied shut.

The scientists who tracked female alligators in the Rockefeller Refuge found that the females headed away from open water after mating. Adult females, they discovered, have a range of about forty acres. When it came time to build nests, the females journeyed into the parts of the marsh that were thickest. The alligator appears not to nest in salt marsh, but in brackish and freshwater marshes. The trek to the nesting place is one the female makes alone. She walks slowly through the marsh grass with her body held off the ground. Her tail drags behind her and crushes the grass she has pushed aside, leaving an easily-seen trail. Often she follows the same trail other females have traveled at this season for many years. By June she has moved to a water-filled pothole in the dense part of the marsh.

National Park Service scientists studied nesting alligators in the Shark River Valley of the Everglades. All the females they observed nested near water holes. The nests, however, were built in the saw grass. Networks of trails led from the water to the nests. Where the saw grass meets the mangroves, the scientists found, the gators nest not far from the mangrove-lined creeks. Even so, the nests themselves are built in the saw grass.

Around the pothole, the wire grass and other marsh plants grow thickly. A few hundred yards off, a stand of cypress trees reaches for the sky. Its branches are the site of a rookery of herons and egrets. The birds seem constantly aflutter, with plumes waving in the soft breeze.

The female gator, however, pays no attention to the birds. About fifteen feet from the water, she begins to build her nest. With her huge jaws she tears up mouthfuls of grasses, reeds, leaves, and twigs. These she drops on the ground in a pile. Time passes and still she works, scooping up dirt and muck with the plants, making the pile larger. But then she stops. She looks around for a moment, and suddenly crawls away from her pile. At a spot a few dozen feet away, she again begins to rip up plants and dirt. For some unknown reason, she has given up her first nest.

Sometimes a female alligator begins nests in several different spots. However, she finishes only one nest. No one knows why she builds the false nests. Is it to lure raccoons and other creatures, who might eat her eggs, away from the real nest? Or does she just try several spots until one satisfies her most? Often the female may build her nest over the remains of one used in earlier years. In

A female gator stays by her nest in the Louisiana marshes.

some places one nest is piled on top of another, year after year. These piles may be three or four feet high.

The job of building the nest takes as long as two weeks. The female works hard for many hours each day. She tears up plants, and rips branches and leaves from trees. All go on her nest pile. More and more plants and dirt are added. Still she works. Once in a while she leaves the nest, but she does not go far, usually no more than a half mile. Sometimes she goes to the water. When she returns to the nest she is dripping. As she crawls back and forth over the nest, the water dampens the pile. The weight of her body packs it down. When clumps of plants and dirt fall from the pile, she gathers them up with her mouth. She dumps the loose material higher on the pile. With her tail, sides, feet, and mouth the female shapes the pile into a cone. Eventually it is five feet across and two feet high. When the female finishes the mound, she backs over it. Her strong hind feet scoop out a hole a foot wide and a foot deep in the top of the cone. She will lay her eggs in the hole.

After she digs the hole, however, the female alligator may wait many hours, even days, before she starts to lay her eggs. Scientists do not understand why or for what she waits. But sooner or later she climbs to the top of the nest and is ready. Her scaly body presses down on the damp pile of plants. Moving with care, she places a hind leg on either side of the hole she has dug in the top of the pile.

Nearby a bullfrog calls. But the alligator pays no heed. Not far off, an eastern diamondback rattlesnake strikes at a rice rat. The rat stiffens, kicks its feet for a few seconds, and dies. The snake moves in to swallow its meal. On the other side of the water hole, a male raccoon noses about the water looking for a fat crayfish to eat. Far across the marshes, a mother raccoon leads her four young from their den. The male raccoon has never seen the young, although he is their father. It is the female's task to care for them alone.

All around the alligator's nest, the cycle of life and death goes on in the marsh. Meanwhile, the female gator settles over the hole. 48

Her tail lifts slightly, and she begins to lay her eggs. One by one they fall between her hind legs into the hole. As each egg drops, it brushes against her legs, which break its fall. The egg is oblong, about three inches long and an inch wide. Its shell is whitish. By the time the female is finished, as many as five dozen eggs may lie inside the hole atop the nest. Once the last egg drops into the nest the female carefully nudges some of the plant matter over the eggs, closing the hole.

It takes nine weeks in the nest before the young gators hatch. As the plant matter in the pile rots, it gives off heat. The heat incubates the eggs. At the same time the nest shields the eggs from sharp changes of temperature outside. Many things can go wrong for the young gators in the nest. It could become too hot, or too cold, for them to hatch. If the nest dries out, they may not hatch either, nor may they hatch if the nest is flooded. Raccoons or feral hogs might find the nest, dig it up, and eat the eggs or young.

Little by little, scientists are learning what kind of nest conditions are best for young alligators. But it will be a long time before they fully understand the gator's nesting needs. Year after year, in many different places, nests must be examined. Conditions around the nests must be observed carefully. All of the information from these studies must be assembled. Even though the job is difficult, however, a good start has been made. Many nests have been studied by scientists in Florida and in the Rockefeller Refuge.

Scientists at the Refuge searched for nests from the air. They flew back and forth, in a helicopter above the waving marsh grasses, looking for heaps of plant matter that might be nests. When they spotted one, the searchers radioed its location to men on the ground. Riding in a marsh buggy, they plowed through the water and grass to the site of the nest.

In one study a thermometer was placed inside each nest. It recorded the temperatures within the nest while the young alligators were developing there. Another thermometer was placed outside each nest to record the temperature of the air. The temperature of the air around the nests changed often. On some days it was very

Scientists at Rockefeller Wildlife Refuge mark the location of an alligator nest.

cool, on others warm. Such sharp temperature changes could have endangered young alligators. However, inside the nest the young were shielded from the effects of changes in the weather. The temperature within the nests usually remained at an even level. It averaged about 83°F.

The scientists also strung a trip wire across each nest. It was set so that the female alligator would trigger it by crawling over the nest. Each time the wire was triggered, it was recorded on electronic equipment. The recordings would tell something about how much time the female spent around the nest. Some of the females triggered the wire at their nest many times. Others, however, tripped it only a few times.

This is not surprising, however. Not all female alligators behave alike during nesting. Some females charge and hiss at intruders who come too near the nest. Others do not guard the nest at all.

Some females remain close to the nest most of the time; others wander far from it. All nesting females, however, often travel to nearby water, to drink and keep cool.

The female alligator may not know that by building her special kind of nest she is helping her kind survive. Nest-building is part of the automatic pattern of alligator life that has worked well for ages. As long as it continues to work well, the alligator will survive.

When man interferes with the environment, however, even a time-tested way of life may fail. An animal's pattern for living fits in with its environment and the regular cycles that occur in the environment. If man alters the environment, the animal may not be able to cope with the new conditions. In the Everglades, for example, the cycle of high water and drought has been changed. Water has been dammed up within large areas of marsh. These areas have been set aside to store water from rainfall until it is needed for farms and cities. When it rains the water does not naturally drain out of these areas as in the past. The water level rises in these areas. They are flooded with much more water than used to flow into them.

Since the rainy season in the Everglades begins in June, the stored water rises in the storage areas at about the time the alligators are nesting. An alligator may build its nest on land that is dry before the rains begin, but which is flooded as the water rises. Many of the nests and young in the water-storage areas are destroyed in this way. One summer, scientists checked one part of a water-storage area during early June and found seventeen gator nests. The level of the water in the area was only eight inches. A month later, however, the water was more than two feet deep. Sixteen of the nests, which had been dry, now were flooded. Scientists say that by storing water the authorities (the Army Corps of Engineers and the Central and Southern Florida Control District) may be causing an unnatural pattern of flooding in the Everglades. They warn that it might prevent the alligators in the storage areas from successfully hatching young.

51

When nesting conditions are right, however, the young are ready to hatch in about sixty days. The baby gator lies curled tightly within the shell that has enclosed it. The baby's tail and head touch its belly. As hatching nears, the little animal grows rapidly. Cracks begin to split the shell lengthwise, from one end to the other. Other cracks branch out from them until there is a spidery network on the face of the shell. The shell breaks and opens just above the young gator's head.

The little alligator still is not free. For within the shell is a thin but tough skin. It encloses the youngster. The young alligator, however, has a tool for cutting open the skin. It is called an egg tooth. The egg tooth is a small, sharp bump on the end of the baby gator's snout. (It is also present in most birds and many other reptiles.) By moving its head, the young alligator slices open the skin with the egg tooth. After the gator hatches, the egg tooth disappears. Scientists are not sure whether it shrinks away or falls off the snout.

When the young alligators are ready to hatch, cracks develop in the shells.

It may take as long as a week before the young gator's snout peeps from the shell. But the baby is buried deep within the mound of rotting material that has protected it for so long. Most young gators cannot dig their way out. They need help. This help comes from the mother. She is nearby and hears when the young gators begin to make soft grunts. Sometimes the mother gator may answer her young who are calling within the nest. The noise she makes sounds something like the grunt of a pig.

Opening her jaws, the mother moves to the top of the nest. She bites huge chunks from the top of the rotting pile. Soon she has shoveled away enough vegetation to uncover the young. For the first time the young gator pokes its head from the shell. It waits a few minutes, then wriggles out.

The youngster is slightly over eight inches long. It weighs only two ounces. Its underside is whitish. White markings are visible on its black sides and upper parts. As the gator grows, the white markings will turn yellow. The young gator's belly is puffed out— it still is filled with the remains of the yolk on which it fed while in the shell.

Once it has hatched, the young gator almost immediately heads for water. In the Everglades the nest may be in shallow water. In other places the nest may be several feet away from water. Scientists long have puzzled over how the young gators know in which direction the water lies. However they do it, the young gators are very accurate.

Although the young gator is small, it immediately is plunged into the life-and-death struggle of nature. It must kill to live. And it must escape being killed by creatures who want to eat it. Great blue herons, raccoons, king snakes and cottonmouths gobble up the little gators. Once they scuttle into the water, black bass, bullfrogs, and snapping turtles prey on them. There are many stories about the mother alligator protecting her young, but scientists disagree on whether they are true. It seems as though some females may protect their young while others do not. Often, however, an adult alligator will protect a young gator even if the baby is not one of its own offspring. When a small gator is handled roughly, it utters a shrill call. It repeats the call again and again. The call warns other young alligators. At the same time, it will draw almost any big gator that hears it. The adult seems to act automatically. Its behavior seems triggered by the call of the youngster. Such behavior is another part of the pattern by which the alligator lives.

Even though adult alligators may protect the young, many baby alligators are eaten soon after hatching. Young alligators in turn eat smaller animals. With sideswipes of the jaws, the young gators snap at minnows, small crayfish, and other small water creatures. Like the adults, the young take food with the sides of the mouth. As they grow, they prey on larger animals—leopard frogs, cricket frogs, tree frogs, large minnows and crayfish.

Scientists of the Florida Game and Fresh Water Fish Commission examined thirty-six young alligators to learn what they were eating. The alligators lived in a canal in the Everglades. Their stomachs were full of snails that were common in the canal. Many small fish, crayfish and giant water bugs also had been eaten by the young gators.

Larger alligators feed on many different animals. They eat large numbers of turtles. The shell of the turtle offers no problem to a hungry alligator. The gator's powerful jaws can crush the shell of even a large turtle. Alligators also feed heavily on gars. These large fish compete with bass and other sport fish. By eating large numbers of gars, the alligator does the fisherman a favor. Fewer gars mean more sport fish. In places where alligators have been killed off, gars have multiplied and have become pests. Bullfrogs, which sometimes swallow baby gators, are easy prey for large alligators.

This nest has been opened, but the young alligators have not yet left it.

So are many snakes, including the big, venomous cottonmouth. Norway rats, marsh rabbits, rice rats, and muskrats disappear into the jaws of alligators. Alligators also prey on some birds—ducks, herons and egrets—but not as much as many people think. Even big gators eat crayfish and blue crabs. Alligators that live on the northwestern coast of Florida move from fresh marshes into salt marshes in the summer to feed on crabs. Many alligators use the same trails through the marsh grass. Some of the trails are well worn by alligators using them time after time.

The young alligators begin to hunt for food soon after they enter the water. It is thought that once in the water, the young gators spread out. Not all scientists who study the alligator, however, accept this. Some researchers say that young alligators stay in the water, near where they were hatched, for two years, possibly three years. It may be that where food is abundant, and water plentiful, the young gators scatter. But where water is scarce, many young gators may stay together in a small water hole. In the orange groves on Merritt Island, ditches hold most of the open water. In one ditch, during the spring, I saw more than a dozen young alligators together. Some were from last summer's hatching. Several were even older—they had hatched almost two years before.

Often adult alligators are found in the same holes with young. Are the adults the mothers of the young? Many people long have believed so. Recently, however, some alligator-watchers have questioned this. If a big gator is found in a water hole with young, does it mean that they are a family? Or are the adult and young unrelated? These are some of the questions about alligators that have not been answered to everyone's satisfaction.

Many alligators in places such as the Everglades and the Okefenokee Swamp dig large holes in which to live. Some of these "gator holes" may be twelve feet deep and several yards wide. They are shaped like washbasins and quickly fill with water. They shelter the alligator during dry spells and in cold weather. Young alligators often take advantage of holes dug by larger ones. Many

56

young may use an adult alligator's hole as their home. Both young and the adult may be found in the hole. This does not mean, however, that they are related.

In the soft marsh of places such as the Okefenokee the alligator can easily dig a large hole. The gator noses into the soft, oozy muck and pushes it aside with its flanks and tail. Gradually, a saucer-shaped hole forms around the alligator. The muck and marsh plants pile up around the edge of the hole. In the Everglades, the alligator often finds a ready-made hole. Limestone, such as that which lies under the Everglades, is pocked with holes and caverns. Often all the Everglades gator has to do is dig out a shallow covering of muck from a hole already formed in the limestone.

Once the hole is dug, the alligator keeps it clear of weeds and muck. The gator bites and tears away plants that may begin to grow in the water of the hole. If plant growth is heavy in a gator hole, it is certain that the alligator no longer lives there.

The gator hole is an important part of the chain of life in the Everglades. Plants of many kinds take root in the muck pushed up around the rim of the hole. Here the heaped soil from the bottom is rich and the plants grow tall and thick. Seeds of the willow ride the wind over the glades and fall on the bank of mud around the hole. They sprout and begin to grow. Their roots send strong fingers through the mud. They provide a framework for the bank, holding it together. As the willows grow, they form a green wall around the hole. As time passes and the willows grow bigger, other plants also rise around the hole. As long as the water is not salty, the large brown leaves of the alligator flags wave on stems ten feet high. Arrowhead and ferns grow thickly. Wax myrtle, buttonbush, and red bay add to the green wall around the hole. Beneath these trees are trails pushed through the greenery by the alligator as it comes and goes from the hole.

Birds of many kinds find the trees at the rim of the hole fine for nesting. Their droppings fall on the soil below. It becomes even richer and the plants in turn grow more lushly. When floods send

When a drought occurs in the Everglades, the gator hole is the last reservoir of water.

water from nearby sloughs spilling into the hole, bass and sunfish may arrive there.

It is in time of drought, however, that the gator holes are most important. The gator holes then are filled largely with ground-water. They are deep enough so that, even in dry periods, water remains in their centers. In many holes the alligators dig a tunnel deep under one side. So when the glades dry up, the gator holes serve as reservoirs.

During the end of winter and in early spring, the gator holes are a source of life-giving water. The rains have not fallen since October. All around, the glades are dry. The wading-bird colonies have young in them by early spring. Because the water is very low, the adult birds can catch many fish, frogs and other small water creatures for their hungry young. These small aquatic animals have come to the gator hole. It is just about the only deep patch of water in the dry prairie. Otters, raccoons, wading birds, and other large animals come to the hole for water and to feed on the smaller creatures. The alligators in the hole eat some of the turtles, birds and other animals that have gathered there. But the presence of the hole and its water keep many more creatures alive. For every bird the gator kills, ten more will live because of the gator hole. In fact, the drop in numbers of Everglades wading birds may be due to the decrease in gator holes.

Every few years the Everglades experience an especially bad drought. Then the holes are vital. If the alligator disappeared from south Florida, engineers would have to blast out artificial gator holes in the Everglades. In the bad droughts the gator holes are the only haven for life in the glades, for then the watery wilderness becomes a desert. The saw grass rattles dryly in the hot sun. A hot wind blows through the grasses. This is the time when a spark can set miles of saw grass on fire, sending smoke billowing more than 5,000 feet into the air. The sloughs are empty of water. The mud on their bottoms is dry and marked with a network of cracks. Gar, bass, and sunfish flop out their lives in the few small puddles that remain. Soon these dry out too.

Only in the gator hole is there water. Even in the hole, however, the water level has dropped. The water that remains is shallow, syrupy, and green. Scum covers it. But under the scum, life teems. Bass and bluegills swim near the surface. Gar and catfish lie close to the dark bottom ooze. Leopard frogs and pig frogs sit in the green slime at the water's edge. Larger birds and mammals come to feed on the frogs and fish. Snails burrow into the mud at the bottom of the hole. Overhead, vultures circle, wings outspread. They drop down from the sky to feed on the dead and dying animals around the hole. The water itself is thick with tiny bits of life. In the water are diatoms, protozoans, and little crustaceans. Some are too small for the eye alone to see. Although they are small, these bits of life are the first link in the food chain. They are the food of slightly larger organisms. These in turn fill the stomachs of big-

59

ger animals. And so it goes on, link by link, until the chain reaches the largest animals, including the alligator. Therefore, by building water holes in which the smallest organisms of the Everglades live, the gator has animals on which to prey.

Eventually, the rains return. The raindrops spatter on the hard, cracked slough beds. The dry crust turns to mud under the wet hammering of the rain. The sloughs fill with water once more. A shimmering carpet of water again covers the saw-grass prairie. The brown vegetation greens. Frogs call from newly made puddles. The deer lick the wet drops from their noses. In the gator hole the water level rises. Soon it overflows. The creatures that have found shelter in the hole spread out over the Everglades. They multiply. The gator, which has spent the worst part of the drought in the deepest cranny of the hole, floats like a log in the water. The Everglades marshland is alive once more.

The gator hole is common in southern Florida. But elsewhere in gator country, alligators dig few such basin-shaped holes. Instead, they often tunnel into the banks of streams and other places where the earth is soft. Sometimes the tunnels collapse and turn into saucerlike holes. Usually, however, the gator's burrow disappears into the ground. Some burrows may reach sixty feet long. They may not be built in a place where water remains year-round. North of Florida, however, most places where the gator digs its burrow flood in winter. And winter is about the only time the alligator uses the burrow. When the weather cools, the gator retreats deep into the tunnel it has dug.

In the Everglades, the deep water of the gator hole remains warm even during brief cold snaps. Everglades gators have no need of burrows. Some alligators that live in large lakes also seem not to use burrows. The water in the lakes, if not too far north, stays warm enough for the alligator to survive the winter without going into a burrow.

In southern South Carolina, several alligators live in a very unusual pond. Its water is summer-warm even in the middle of a winter ice storm. The pond is on the Savannah River Plant of the United States Atomic Energy Commission. Atomic fuel is made at the plant, which covers three hundred square miles. Water is flushed through pipes to keep the atomic reactors cool. When the water leaves the reactor, it takes a great amount of heat with it. Some of the heat is lost as it passes through a canal. More is lost in a pond into which the canal empties, but the water is still too hot for most water animals. At the end of this pond the water passes over a dam into the pond in which the alligators live. Just below the dam the water stays warm year-round. But it is not too warm for fish, which live there and grow very large. Nor is it too warm for alligators. In fact, it seems to make it easier for the pond's alligators to survive the winter.

During the winter in almost all parts of the alligator's range except southern Florida, the pace of gator life slows down. Cold weather slows the body activity of reptiles. The gator crawls into its burrow during the coldest time. It does not eat, and it hardly moves. It was once thought that the gator hibernates in cold weather, but this does not seem to be true. Instead, the gator seems

During periods of drought, slough beds in the Everglades dry out and crack.

to become dormant for the coldest periods. When it is dormant, the alligator can stay under water for many hours. Normally, gators submerge only for a quarter hour or so. Warm days may bring it out of its burrow, although it may not feed. Rockefeller Refuge scientists have found that big male gators winter in the open waters of large canals. Researchers believe males lie on the bottom five to ten feet below the surface. Females seem to go to dens in isolated parts of the marsh.

At the lake in the Savannah River Plant, the alligators live far from the dam and the warm water in the summer. Scientists at the plant, however, noticed that in winter the gators disappear from their summer quarters. Shortly afterward, alligators turn up below the dam, where the warm water flows. They believe that the gators spend their time in the cooler parts of the lake in summer. When the weather becomes cold, they travel to the warm water instead of holing up in burrows.

Several years ago a swamp existed on the site of the lake. Before the swamp was flooded, a handful of gators lived there. Now more than a hundred alligators swim in the lake. These may be the descendants of the gators that inhabited the old swamp. Many of the alligators in the lake have grown over eight feet long. Turtles in the lake grow very large. In fact, they are much larger than turtles from nearby ponds and streams. The year-round warm water may produce extra food for the turtles and alligators to eat. In addition, the gators may feed all winter, and grow. If they burrowed into the ground, they probably would not feed.

This is another part of the alligator's life that needs much study before we really can understand the way of the gator.

The Future of the Gator

By the year 2000, many kinds of wild animals alive today will have vanished from the earth. Many others will exist only in zoos or parks. Each year there is less and less space on the earth for wild animals. This is because each year more and more people populate our planet. More people means that the earth's resources are used up more quickly; forests are cut, marshes are drained, grasslands are turned to farmland. More people also means that there is more pollution of the water and air. Possibly, however, man will learn to live with the natural world. If so, mankind will live in a way that leaves room for forests, marshes, grasslands, and the animals that live in them. Possibly, too, mankind will stop hunting wild animals that are few in number. However, it must happen soon, or it will be too late for many wild creatures.

Will there be tigers in the year 2000? Will the great whales still rove the seas? Will the bellow of the gator still thunder in the southern wetlands? It all depends on what happens in the next few years. If mankind does not learn to live with nature, many wild animals will soon be only a memory.

Among the animals most in danger are the large predators. For some reason, man seems always to wage war on big predatory animals—even if they do not threaten humans. The gator, one of the largest predators in North America, has long been a victim of this war. It may seem odd to say that the alligator is in danger of extinction. There are many gators living in our southern wetlands. However, an animal is not always safe from extinction just because it is numerous. A species of animal might number in the millions. But suppose it lived only on one island, and only in the island's forests. Suppose the forests were cut for lumber and to make room for farmland and cities. What would happen to that species? Its home would be destroyed. And because it lived on an island it would have no other place to go. It would die out.

One hundred years ago, hundreds of millions of passenger pigeons darkened the sky as they migrated over the eastern United States. Fifty years ago there were no passenger pigeons left. The passenger pigeon is as extinct as the dinosaur.

People once thought there was no end to the supply of passenger pigeons. They hunted the pigeons without stop. Pigeons were shot as they flew overhead. They were clubbed in their nests. Millions of pigeons were slaughtered. The woodlands where the pigeons nested were cut. Yet people were surprised when, finally, the number of pigeons dwindled. By the time people realized that the pigeons were in danger, not enough of these birds were left to continue their kind. Today, scientists are learning to breed wild animals in zoos. The passenger pigeon might have been saved in modern zoos. But now it is too late for the passenger pigeon.

There is no kind of animal that today cannot be hunted out of existence by mankind. Numbers mean nothing in the face of today's hunting methods. Possibly more than a million alligators live in the wild. Millions of other Crocodilians live in other parts of the world. But all of them are in danger of extinction. How can this be, when so many Crocodilians exist? As long as some people will pay money for Crocodilian hides, other people will hunt Crocodilians. And as long as the hunters can sell the hides, they will kill as many Crocodilians as they can. Today two million Crocodilians are killed each year for their hides. Millions more would be killed without laws to regulate Crocodilian hunting and selling of the leather. Without such laws, all wild American alligators would be killed in a very short time.

As long as good laws protect the American alligator it probably will continue to exist. That is, however, if the wetlands in which the alligator lives continue to exist. Some of these wetlands are in parks and preserves like the Everglades National Park. But others belong to private owners. How can we be sure that private land-owners will not build homes, industries or farms on the wetland homes of alligators? One answer might be to allow the private landowners to hunt some of the alligators and sell the hides under strict rules. Only small numbers of alligators could be killed. Hunting would not be allowed to interfere with alligator breeding. Enough alligators would be left alone to continue their kind. Hunters who did not obey the rules would be guilty of crime. If the rules were followed, the private landowners could gain profit from having alligators on their land. Therefore they would preserve the wetlands and the alligators. This may be an answer to saving alligators on private land. Some scientists think so. Others believe that any hunting of the gator is wrong.

Baby alligators should not be kept as pets, since this takes them out of the breeding population. Besides, gators grow too large to keep at home. Many states have banned the sale of baby alligators and baby caimans, which often are sold as alligators.

As long as alligator hides can be sold for money, some people will buy them. This means that there may always be hunters who will risk not obeying the law to kill alligators. Many people who are trying to save the alligator believe there is a way to produce alligator hides without hunting. Why not raise alligators on farms, they ask? That way, alligator hides could be obtained without hunting. If a farmer could supply hides, there would be no need to kill wild alligators.

65   Before alligators can be farmed, however, scientists must learn

more about how they live. Farmers must learn how to make alligators grow rapidly. They must find ways that they can afford for feeding and housing alligators. They must learn how to make alligators breed in captivity as readily as they do in the wild. And young alligators must be hatched and reared on the farms. If all this happens it may be possible to farm alligators for their hides, and even for their meat.

At the same time, however, many people believe there is no need for man to wear the skins of wild animals in today's world. Human beings can get along without alligator shoes and handbags. Plenty of other materials besides gator hide can be used for these items. Is there really any reason, besides profit, to hunt the alligator for its hide?

The American alligator needs human help if it is to survive.

What is the future of the gator? Should gators be hunted under strict rules? Should gators be farmed? Should they be left entirely alone to live as they did in the days before man? Possibly the answer lies in all of these ideas. If alligators are left alone they could become too numerous in some places; hunters might be needed to thin their numbers. If gators can be farmed, wild alligators will be much more safe, for it will be easier to get hides from captive alligators. If wildernesses like the Everglades National Park are preserved, some alligators can continue to live as they have for millions of years.

Above all, humans must remember that both man and gator share the same system of life. It is the system to which all living things on our planet belong. Man has changed the system in many ways. Some changes have been for the good, and many for the bad. Yet although man can change the system, he cannot control nature. Man must learn to live with nature if man himself is to survive. If man preserves wild creatures like the gator, it is a sign that he truly is learning the lesson.

Credits

Front cover photograph courtesy of New York Zoological Society.
Back cover photograph courtesy of Rockefeller Wildlife Refuge.
Photographs on pages *4, 10, 33,* and *35* courtesy of Georgia Game and Fish Commission.
Map on page *19* by Dan Dickas.
Photographs on pages *7, 8, 16, 21, 22, 24,* and *27* courtesy of National Park Service.
Photographs on pages *36, 37, 39, 40, 43, 47, 50, 52,* and *55* courtesy of Rockefeller Wildlife Refuge.
Photographs on title page and page *43* by Edward R. Ricciuti.
Photographs on pages *58* and *61* by William Powers.
Photograph on page *66* courtesy of New York Zoological Society.

For further reading

Bellairs, Angus d'A., *Reptiles.* 2nd ed.
   New York: Hillary House, 1968.

Bridges, William, *The Bronx Zoo Book of Wild Animals.*
   New York: New York Zoological Society and Golden Press, 1968.

Leviton, Allan, *Amphibians and Reptiles of North America.*
   Garden City, N.Y.: Doubleday, 1971.

Neill, Wilfred T., *The Last of the Ruling Reptiles.*
   New York: Columbia University Press, 1971.

Niering, William A., *The Life of the Marsh.*
   New York: McGraw-Hill, 1967.

Smith, Frances C., *The First Book of Swamps and Marshes.*
   New York: Franklin Watts, Inc., 1969.

Index